Waves at Work

SRA

Columbus, OH

SRAonline.com

 SRA

Send all inquiries to this address:
SRA/McGraw-Hill
4400 Easton Commons
Columbus, OH 43219-6188

ISBN: 978-0-07-611739-0
MHID: 0-07-611739-1

1 2 3 4 5 6 7 8 9 RRS 13 12 11 10 09 08 07

The **McGraw·Hill** Companies

You are at a football game when an excited group of fans suddenly stands up. They raise and lower their arms and then they quickly sit back down. Without a pause, the people next to them do the same thing. Before long everyone in the stadium has been a part of the "wave." What is the reason that we call this movement a wave? How is it like other waves? How is it different?

What is a wave? There are different kinds of waves. What do all waves have in common? How do waves behave?

What do you think of when you think of a wave? Maybe you imagine the waves that you are likely to see on a lake or in the ocean. Perhaps you think about the waves that spread out over the surface of the water when you drop a rock in a puddle.

Waves are all around you, including many that you never think about. For example, what do you see across the room? The light that helps you see across the room comes to you in waves. How loud is your CD player? All sound, including music, travels in waves.

Water, light, and sound waves are different, however. Do they have anything in common? Why is each of these considered a wave?

All waves have two things in common. First a wave moves through its environment. Ocean waves move through the water around them, and sound waves move through air. Light waves can move through both empty space and some types of matter. Matter is anything that takes up space and has mass. Air and water are both examples of matter.

Second, a wave carries energy from one place to another. Because a wave moves, it has energy. Have you ever had a sand castle knocked down by an ocean wave? A water wave transfers energy.

Think about the wave of fans in the football stadium. The human wave in the stadium models a type of wave called a transverse wave. A transverse wave is a wave that vibrates sideways when compared with the direction in which it is traveling. The stadium wave vibrates up and down as it moves forward through the stadium. All electromagnetic waves, including visible light waves, are transverse waves.

Transverse waves have different parts. The highest part of a wave is called the crest of the wave. The lowest part of a wave is called the trough of the wave. An imaginary line halfway between the crest and the trough is called the rest position.

You can model a transverse wave. Imagine that you are holding one end of a jump rope and your friend is holding the other end. You move your end of the rope up and down, and the rope begins to vibrate, or move in waves. Each wave has a crest and a trough as it moves along the rope to your friend.

Suppose that you tie a ribbon to the middle of the rope. As each wave passes the ribbon, the ribbon moves up and down. Sometimes the ribbon is at the highest part of a wave, and sometimes it is at the lowest part. Sometimes it is in between. However the ribbon does not move along the rope as the wave does.

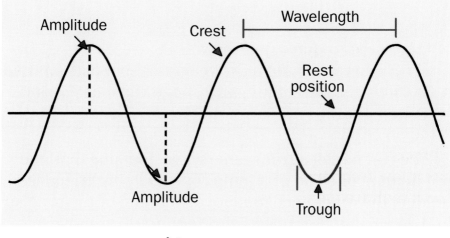

A transverse wave

Transverse waves have other properties too. The length of one wave is called the wave's wavelength. Wavelength is the distance from the highest part of one wave to the highest part of a wave behind it or in front of it, or from crest to crest. It is also the distance from the lowest part of one wave to the lowest part of the previous or next wave, or from trough to trough.

The amplitude of the wave is the distance from the rest position to the highest part of the wave. Amplitude can also be measured as the distance from the rest position to the lowest part of the wave. Very tall waves have more energy. Shorter waves have less energy.

Suppose that you counted the number of transverse waves that go by in ten seconds. A high number of waves might go by, or a low number of waves might go by. The number of waves that go by in an amount of time is the frequency of the wave.

Frequency is related to wavelength. Suppose that two waves move at the same speed. If one wave has a long wavelength, only a few waves will pass in ten seconds. If the other wave has a short wavelength, more waves will pass in ten seconds. A wave with a long wavelength has a low frequency. A wave with a short wavelength has a high frequency.

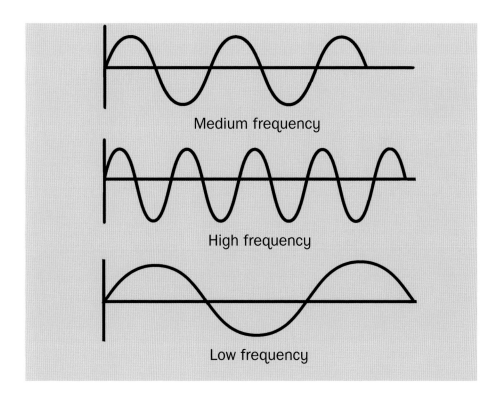

Medium frequency

High frequency

Low frequency

You know that light lets you see across the room. Light moves as transverse waves. What other waves are transverse waves?

If you want to quickly warm up leftover pizza, what do you use? You might use a microwave oven. Microwaves are also transverse waves. Microwaves cook food by transferring energy to the water in food. The microwave oven was named after microwaves.

Where is the remote? Who had it last? Many remote controls use waves of a certain frequency to communicate with your television or DVD player. These rays are also transverse waves.

In addition to waves of visible light, the sun sends other high-energy transverse waves to Earth. Ultraviolet waves, for example, can cause sunburn by damaging skin cells. Because they damage cells, these waves can also be used to kill germs that may cause disease.

Have you ever had an X-ray to find out whether you broke a bone or whether your teeth are free of cavities? X-rays are also transverse waves. They have so much energy that they easily pass through objects. The results are pictures of what the rays passed through. X-rays are also used to look into your luggage at airport security checkpoints.

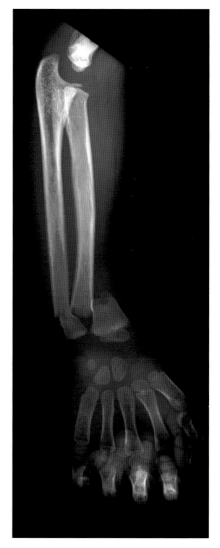

X-rays help find injuries.

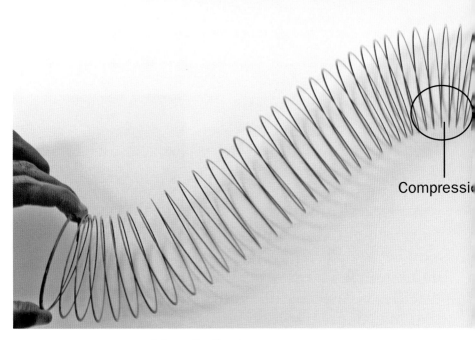

Compressi[o]

A longitudinal wave

A water wave is another kind of wave. Think about a calm lake. If you toss a rock into the water, the waves move outward from where the rock went in. Energy is being transferred outward in all directions.

A water wave is a surface wave. A surface wave is very much like a transverse wave. The water moves up and down. The wave moves forward. A surface wave is not a pure transverse wave, though. A water wave moves forward, but the water in the wave also moves back and forth a little bit as it moves up and down.

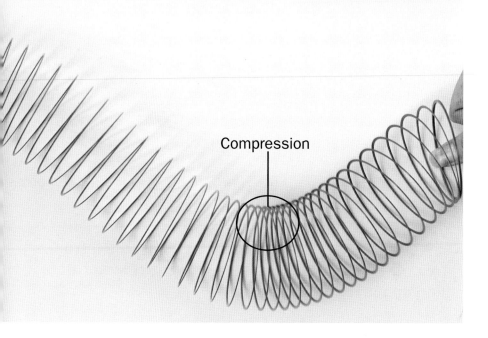

Compression

Another type of wave is called a longitudinal wave. Longitudinal waves also move energy as the wave moves. Longitudinal waves include sound waves and certain types of waves caused by earthquakes.

You can model longitudinal waves by using a spring toy. Lay the spring toy on the floor. Hold one end. Stretch out the spring and have a friend hold the other end. While still holding the end of the spring, bunch together several of the coils with your hand. Then turn them loose.

You can see that an area of bunched up, squeezed-together coils, called a compression, moves down the spring. Longitudinal waves are sometimes called compressional waves.

Think again about the spring toy model of a longitudinal wave. Longitudinal waves vibrate in the same direction that the wave travels. You can see that some coils are squeezed closer together and some coils are stretched farther apart.

Longitudinal waves cause particles to move closer together and then move farther apart. They do not have high and low parts as transverse waves do. The wavelength of a longitudinal wave is the distance from one area of bunched-up particles to the next area of bunched-up particles.

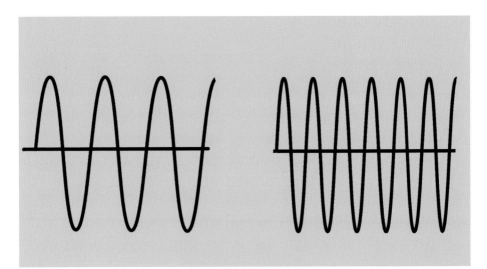

Longitudinal waves

The frequency of a longitudinal wave is the number of waves that pass in a given amount of time. Frequency is measured by finding the number of areas of bunched-up particles that go by in the chosen time period.

Remember that the amplitude of a transverse wave is a measure of how much energy the wave has. The amplitude of a longitudinal wave cannot be measured in the same way because the wave does not have high parts and low parts. The amplitude of a longitudinal wave is measured by how closely the particles in the wave are pushed together. The more the particles are pushed together, the more energy the wave has.

Sound waves are longitudinal waves. When something causes a noise, it disturbs the air around it, and this disturbance travels through the air as sound waves.

Sound waves have properties that describe them. Do all band instruments sound alike? The tuba has a low sound. The flute has a high sound. The pitch of a sound is how low or how high it is. Pitch is a property of a sound wave.

High-frequency sounds have a high pitch. Low-frequency sounds have a low pitch. A tuba has a low pitch. A tuba produces low-frequency sound waves. A flute has a high pitch. The sound waves it makes have high frequency.

What is the difference in your friend's voice when she whispers and when she yells? The difference is the sound's strength. The strength of a sound depends on how much the particles are pushed together in the wave. The particles of air are pushed very close together when your friend yells. It also depends on how far the listener is from the source of the sound.

Loudness is not the same as strength. Loudness depends on the person hearing the sound. Two people might hear the same sound with different loudness.

Waves have speed. How fast do waves move? Light waves move fastest through space because there is no matter in the air. The speed of light has a value of about 187,000 miles per second. This is the fastest speed that anything can have.

When light waves enter matter, the waves slow down. The light slows down because it is affected by the particles of matter. Light is slowed slightly by gases. It moves a bit slower in liquids. Light waves usually travel most slowly through clear solids. In a diamond, for example, light moves at a mere 77,272 miles per second.

Longitudinal waves, such as sound, can move only through matter. The particles of matter can be pressed together. There are no particles to press together in space. Thus sound waves cannot travel in space. In general, sound waves travel fastest in solids. They are usually slower in liquids. Sound usually has the slowest speeds in gases. In general, sound travels faster in matter that has particles that are closer together.

The table below shows the speed of sound in some different materials. Notice that sound travels much faster in water than it does in air. Sound is also much faster in glass than in water.

Gases	
Material	Meters/Second
Hydrogen	1286
Helium	972
Liquids	
Material	Meters/Second
Water	1493
Methyl Alcohol	1143
Solids	
Material	Meters/Second
Diamond	12000
Rubber	1600

Waves do not always have a clear path; that is, they cannot always travel in a perfectly straight line. How does a wave react when it hits something? When waves hit a surface, they may bounce off.

All types of waves bounce off an object when they cannot pass through or into it. Sound waves echo when they bounce off a wall in a large room. Water waves bounce back when they hit an object in the water. You can see yourself in a mirror because light waves bounce off the mirror. It is a common event to see your reflection in a window. Some waves pass through the window glass. Some waves bounce back.

Waves from one material sometimes bend when they enter a different material. The waves bend because they change speed. Remember that waves travel at different speeds, depending on the material through which they are passing.

Look at the pencil in the photo. Light waves travel at a different speed in air than they do in water. As light waves leave water and enter the air, they bend. This bending of the light waves makes the pencil look as though it is broken at the surface of the water.

A rainbow forms because light waves bend as they pass through small drops of water in the air. Different colors of light bend different amounts.

The many types of waves have some things in common. For example, they carry energy and have wavelength and frequency. When they hit an object, they can bounce off, and when they move into something different, they can bend.

Light waves are transverse waves, which have high and low parts. Light waves can travel through space. Sound waves are longitudinal waves. Matter must be present for a longitudinal wave to form. The waves are made up of places where matter is bunched up and other places where matter is not bunched or is spread apart.

Waves are all around you. Can you hear your teacher talking? Can you see the desk next to yours? Can you see your reflection in something shiny? What kinds of waves do you see and hear?

Vocabulary

environment (in vī' rən mənt) (page 5) *n.* Surroundings.

previous (prē' vē əs) (page 8) *adj.* Earlier.

results (ri zults') (page 11) *n.* Plural form of **result:** What you find out when you do an experiment.

pure (pyo͞or) (page 12) *adj.* Not mixed with anything.

react (rē akt') (page 20) *v.* To act because something has happened.

common (ko' mən) (page 20) *adj.* Happening often, familiar.

Comprehension Focus: Drawing Conclusions

1. You can see your face in a puddle of water. What happens to the light waves that hit the puddle?

2. The frequency of light wave A is greater than the frequency of light wave B. What is true about the wavelengths of the two waves?

Activity: Effects of Waves

Do these activities to show how light bends when it goes from one material into another.

What to Do

1. Add water to the clear glass or cup until it is about half full.
2. Stand the pencil in the glass, point down. What do you observe?
3. Now hold the prism so that sunlight shines through one side and so that the light coming through the prism hits a flat object, such as a wall or a table top.
4. Look at the light that is coming through the prism.
5. Write the things you notice about this light.

What You Need
- Pencil
- Clear glass or cup
- Water
- Glass prism

What Happened

- Explain what you saw when you looked at the pencil in the glass.
- Explain why the light that came through the prism was different from sunlight.

What If

What might you see if light passes through water droplets in the air?